In the Garden

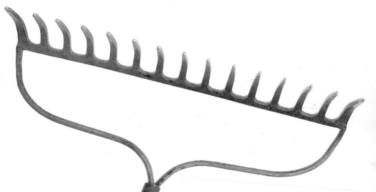

INTRODUCTION

Gardens provide us with outside space in which to play, grow plants and enjoy the sunshine. They are also good places to start learning about nature, as you discover the plants and creatures that live all around us. Gardens can be designed to encourage wildlife, with places for creatures to nest and plants for them to feed on, or they can be used to grow fruit and vegetables. It's really exciting to see a plant growing from a tiny seed into something you can eat, especially if you have planted it and cared for it yourself. And food that has only been picked from the tree or dug out of the ground just a short time before you eat it tastes really good. Some people enjoy gardens full of flowers, and bees like these too, or their gardens have large, lawned areas that are great for playing on.

A garden can be as small as a window box or balcony with some plants in pots, or as large as several football pitches with different areas of trees, planting and interesting features. Some of Britain's grand, stately homes have gardens that are open to the public. These can be many hectares in size, and are often split up into different areas such as woodland, parkland and more formally designed areas, which makes them great places to I-Spy some of the things you may not have in your own garden.

Whatever the size or style of the garden you are looking at, there should be a multitude of things to spot, building your score as you go.

How to use your I-SPY book

As you work through this book, you will notice that the subjects are arranged in groups which are related to the kinds of places where you are likely to find things. You need 1000 points to send off for your i-SPY certificate (see page 64) but that is not too difficult because there are masses of points in every book. Each entry has a star or circle and points value beside it. The stars represent harder to spot entries. As you make each i-SPY, write your score in the circle or star. For entries where there is a question, double your score if you can answer it. Answers are shown on page 63.

PADDLING POOL

Points: 10

A paddling pool is an ideal place to cool down when the weather gets hot.

Points: 15

ROPE SWING

Rope swings are great fun. They are normally fastened to a tree. Be careful not to swing too high – and hold on tight.

SANDPIT

Points: 5

Most children would agree that no garden is complete without a sandpit. This version is neatly enclosed to keep the sand from spreading.

Points: 5

TABLE AND CHAIRS

Garden furniture can be found in a wide variety of styles and materials. This set comes complete with a large parasol to keep the sun off during those hot summer days!

TRAMPOLINE

Points: 10

Some gardens have a bouncy trampoline. This is a great way to get fit and have fun at the same time.

Points: 5

SLIDE

A garden slide can give hours of fun. How fast can you go down the slide? Be careful!

BARBECUE

Points: 5

Food cooked outdoors always tastes fantastic. There are many types of barbecue available.

Points: 10

CHIMENEA

When the evening starts to get chilly, the heat from this safe fire is a great way to keep warm.

HAMMOCK

Points: 20

There is something special about snoozing in a hammock on a summer's afternoon, as long as you can get in that is! How many times have you fallen out?

Points: 15

PATIO HEATER

These may not be a very efficient way of getting warm, but the rosy glow cast by a heater can help prolong that special summer evening.

SWIMMING POOL

Top Spot! **Points: 35**

Maybe you or a friend are lucky enough to have a pool in your garden – what a great way to while away a summer's day.

GREENHOUSE

Points: 15

The transparent ceiling and walls allow the sun to warm the air inside a greenhouse, making it an ideal place to germinate seeds and grow plants. These days many greenhouses have plastic windows instead glass which used to be more common.

Points: 5

WOODEN SHED

All gardens need a shed. It's somewhere to store the garden tools as well as toys and bikes and, of course, the lawn mower.

DOG KENNEL

Top Spot!   Points: 35

If your dog is not allowed in the house he must have one of his own! Your loyal friend deserves a cosy warm place that protects him from the weather.

Points: 30   Top Spot!

TREE HOUSE

Wouldn't it be fun to spend time playing in a house up in a tree? For most people it's just a dream but a tree house can provide hours of fun.

GAZEBO

Points: 15

Most modern gazebos are temporary tent-like structures made from fabric supported on poles. Permanent gazebos are usually made of wood or metal. They create shade on sunny days and provide shelter when it rains.

Points: 15

ARBOUR

You'll often find fragrant climbing plants such as roses or honeysuckle growing up over the sides of these garden alcoves. Arbours usually contain a seat or surround a garden gate, as in the picture.

RHUBARB

Points: 10

This is a tall perennial plant with large, wrinkly leaves and red stems, which are the edible parts. Don't try to eat the leaves as they contain oxalic acid and are therefore poisonous. Its natural season is from March to July.

 Points: 10

CAULIFLOWER

Cauliflowers are difficult to grow as they need a lot of rain and good soil. The white part of a cauliflower is actually the flower - the proper name for it is the curd. Depending on the variety, they can be harvested between early spring and November. Some winter crops are cut between December and March.

BROAD BEAN

Points: 10

This hardy bean can be planted before winter and will burst into life in the spring. Picking usually takes place between May and August. Beware of letting the pods get too big as the beans will become hard.

TOMATO

Points: 5

Tomatoes are easy to grow and come in many different sizes. Surprisingly, not all tomatoes are red. Other colours include orange, yellow, pink, purple and green. Black or white ones are also grown! Crops are generally harvested between July and October.

Points: 10

ONION

Onions are one of the oldest vegetables and are grown in most countries of the world. They are used to flavour savoury food and can be acidic, mild, sweet or even spicy. Crops are ready between July and September.

POTATO

Points: 5

The humble potato is our most popular vegetable and is one of the most versatile. Did you know that the average person in the UK eats over 30 kilos of them every year! Early varieties, lifted in June or July, are known as new potatoes, while the main crop is ready in September.

Points: 15

BRUSSELS SPROUT

These vegetables are a type of small cabbage. They are very good for you as they contain essential vitamins and good quantities of dietary fibre. A useful winter crop, they crop between August and February.

BEETROOT

Points: 15

The red stems and the green leaves help to brighten up the vegetable patch. Their juice contains a dye called betanin, which can leave your hands red for days if you touch them. They can be pulled any time between late spring and autumn.

Points: 15

MARROW

The marrow is actually a fruit (botanically speaking) and is part of a huge family of plants that includes pumpkins, gherkins and courgettes. They can reach gigantic proportions, weighing over 50kg and measuring 130cm (51 inches) long. They are harvested between July and October.

RUNNER BEAN

Points: 10

We eat the green pods and the multi-coloured beans in this country but in America this climbing plant is grown for its beautiful flowers. Supported on a frame, it easily grows to 2m (6.5ft) high. It's ready to pick from July to October.

 Points: 15

PEA

Not many things are as tasty as freshly harvested peas, just popped from their pod. They are generally served cooked but taste great raw. Early crops will be ready in late May while the main crop will be ready from mid-June onwards.

Points: 5

Lettuce can come in six different types and is usually eaten as part of a salad. Like most vegetables, it's good for us and can actually help us to sleep. Normally grown in a greenhouse if it's early or late in the season, or in the open in summer.

CABBAGE

Points: 15

Cabbages can be picked from the garden throughout the year. Varieties are grown all over the world and during most seasons. They are mostly green or white, although a red cabbage is also grown.

Points: 30   **Top Spot!**

ASPARAGUS

Asparagus plants, known as crowns, have been grown around the world since the earliest times for their delicious taste and medicinal properties. We only eat the 'spears', as the young shoots are called. They are cropped between April and June.

GOLDFINCH

Points: 10

Members of this colourful but argumentative section of the finch family are especially drawn to the garden by tiny niger seeds. These seeds are so small that they need to be fed using a special feeder with beak-sized holes.

Points: 15

GREENFINCH

These bright little finches are regulars at the peanut feeders. In winter they form quite large mixed-species feeding flocks with chaffinches and sparrows and even members of the tit family.

SONG THRUSH

Points: 20

Song thrushes are quite rare now in some places. They are a Red List species, which means that they are under threat - they have declined as a breeding species by 50% in 25 years.

Points: 10

HOUSE SPARROW

This cheeky brown bird is a regular visitor to bird tables and will often make its nest in our roof space.

ROBIN

Points: 5

Robins sing loudest in the winter around Christmas time; it's nothing to do with the festivities, they are just staking out territories and getting ready for spring.

Points: 10

STARLING

Starlings are very common and will happily eat almost anything put out for them. In certain special roosting places they gather in huge winter flocks that can be several million strong.

CHAFFINCH

Points: 5

The male in this image is a very colourful bird, a stark contrast to the female, who is various shades of brown. This gives her good camouflage when she is sitting on a clutch of eggs.

 Points: 20

NUTHATCH

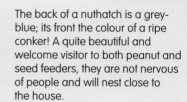

The back of a nuthatch is a grey-blue; its front the colour of a ripe conker! A quite beautiful and welcome visitor to both peanut and seed feeders, they are not nervous of people and will nest close to the house.

BLUE TIT

Points: 5

Blue tits are amazing acrobats. Watch carefully and you may see one hanging upside down by one leg holding a nut in the other while it eats it!

Points: 15

GREAT SPOTTED WOODPECKER

If you are lucky you may hear them drumming on the trunk of a tree or even see one feeding at your bird table. They do, however, have a bad habit of breaking into nest boxes!

CARRION CROW

Points: 10

Your chances of seeing a crow in your garden will depend on how big it is! They are very nervous and don't stay long near people. You are most likely to see them on football fields or parkland.

Points: 5

MAGPIE

While many other garden birds are in decline, magpies are thriving and are now a common visitor to all parts of town and country.

BLACKBERRY

Points: 10

The blackberry is also known as the bramble and it can grow into a large, impenetrable bush. Please be careful of the sharp thorns when you pick the berries in late summer.

 Points: 25

PEAR

Pears are closely related to apples but pear trees are usually found growing in the southern counties of Britain. Your pear will ripen faster if placed next to bananas in a fruit bowl! Trees flower in spring and bear fruit from late August to October.

RASPBERRY

Points: 20

Raspberries bear fruit in summer or autumn depending on the variety. Quite apart from the fact that they are delicious, raspberries are also easy to grow. In fact, they can become quite wild if left unchecked.

Points: 10

APPLE

More than 7500 types of apple have been cultivated and apples are grown all over the world. Fruit is ready to pick each autumn and can be stored in a cold, dry place like the garden shed – just check for rotten ones every few weeks.

PLUM

Points: 20

Greengages, damsons and sloes are all types of plum, but the tree in your garden will probably be a Victoria as it is the most popular of English plums. All contain a hard stone in the centre which contains the seed. If you can see white flowers on a tree in early spring it's probably a member of the plum family. Ready to pick late summer.

Points: 10

STRAWBERRY

Not surprisingly, strawberries are the most popular soft fruit in Britain, yet the season is very short – from mid-May to July.

ROWAN

Points: 15

The rowan is a small deciduous tree that grows between 4–12m (13–39ft) tall. It is easily recognised by the bunches of bright red berries that appear in early autumn, which are loved by birds.

Points: 5

IVY

The common ivy is valued by homeowners as a plant to grow up unsightly fences or ugly structures. It grows quickly and provides a safe place for birds to nest and insects to hibernate.

Points: 20

Common lilac grows as either a tree or shrub, to a height of up to 8m (26ft). It is mainly grown for its beautiful-smelling flowers which, as the name suggests, are lilac in colour although they can also be white. Look out for these in May and June.

BOX HEDGE

Points: 15

Box is a small, sweet-smelling evergreen shrub. It is often used in formal gardens, where it can be clipped into different shapes or used as a low hedge around a flower or herb bed.

Points: 10

PRIVET HEDGE

This is another common hedging plant and is related to the olive. It too is evergreen and can grow tall if neglected, so it really needs to be clipped at least twice a year. It has clumps of tiny white flowers with a distinct aroma, which some people are allergic to.

HONEYSUCKLE

Points: 15

This is a climbing plant that rambles up and over other plants and is often found on the outside of old houses. It flowers profusely and produces the most amazing perfume on summer nights, which attracts pollinating insects.

Points: 5

DAFFODIL

This is the national flower of Wales and one that we all look forward to seeing after a long, cold winter. Its early flowers provide food for bumble bees and other insects emerging from hibernation.

Points: 15

SWEET PEA

This perfumed and colourful member of the pea family will climb to over 2m (6.5ft) tall given support and will flower the whole summer long.

CHRYSANTHEMUM

Points: 10

There are hundreds of different types of chrysanthemum and their flowers are either flat and daisy-like or shaggy and round like this one. Under the right conditions they can be made to flower all year round.

Points: 5

GERANIUM

Although usually referred to as geraniums, the real name of this flower is pelargonium. A very common plant, the flowers come in lots of different colours and some even smell like mint or lemon. The plants are grown commercially – the leaves are harvested and distilled for use in making perfume.

TULIP

Points: 10

Another perennial plant and one of the most common spring-flowering bulbs. The tulip originates from Turkey and was brought to Europe in the mid-sixteenth century.

 Points: 10

PRIMROSE

Primroses are a low-growing plant and by flowering so early in the year they are able to complete their life cycle before being shaded out by taller plants.

SUNFLOWER

Points: 15

This unmistakable, daisy-like flower will grow up to 3m (10ft) high. It prefers dryish soil and, as its name suggests, loves a sunny position in the garden.

Points: 15

SWEET WILLIAM

This short-lived perennial flower can grow up to 75cm (30 inches) tall, which makes it a great favourite with gardeners for the back of the border. The flowers are produced in a dense cluster and have a spicy scent.

FUCHSIA

Points: 15

In some parts of the country this plant has become naturalised and makes a striking appearance in roadside hedges. It is more commonly grown in hanging baskets, ornamental pots or in ordinary flower beds.

 Points: 20

CYCLAMEN

The cyclamen is a lover of cool, damp, shaded places. The leaves are less than 12cm (5 inches) high. It usually flowers in the autumn - try looking under a spreading tree as this is a favourite place to plant then.

ASTER

Points: 15

We know some varieties of aster as Michaelmas daisies – so named because they flower at the time of the Michaelmas festival on 29th September.

Points: 15

GRAPE HYACINTH

The flower that is produced by this bulb may only be 20cm (8 inches) tall but what it lacks in size it makes up for in perfume!

Points: 5

SNOWDROP

The tiny white flowers of the snowdrop herald the start of a new year in the garden. The snow may still be around but here are the first flowers of the year, nodding in the chilly breeze.

WISTERIA

Points: 20

Clouds of flowers hang like bunches of sweet-smelling grapes, often draped along the front of a house. This plant can grow up to 20m (66ft) tall if it has a solid support.

Points: 10

CLIMBING ROSE

These are not really climbers at all but rely on long flexible canes which need to be trained over a supporting frame, usually made of wire. They can grow to about 5m (16ft) high and are capable of repeat flowering throughout the season.

PANSY

Points: 5

Pansies are the result of successful cross-breeding of several species of a wild plant, the viola. The development started in 1813 and has resulted in plants of many colours which are able to flower even during the winter.

Points: 10

ROSE

Grown for their fragrance and beautiful flowers, roses are the traditional flower of many gardens. Although thought of as the 'classic' English flower, cultivated roses were developed from the Eurasian sweetbriar.

CLEMATIS

Points: 20

This is a large group of plants with showy flowers and a climbing habit. They like to keep their roots cool but have their heads in full sun. All the parts of the plant, while pretty, are poisonous. Take care when handling!

Points: 10

The corn or field poppy used to be a more common sight before the development of weedkillers. It is used to this day as a symbol of remembrance, commemorating the bravery of those who fell in the Great War of 1914–1918.

CORNFLOWER

Points: 15

Hardly seen in the wild now due to agricultural intensification, it was once a feature of every field. Luckily, we can grow it in our gardens to attract and feed butterflies and bees.

WHEELBARROW

Points: 10

The first record of a wheelbarrow is from ancient Greece around 405BC! We have been using them ever since. A typical barrow can hold 170 litres.

 Points: 10

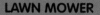
LAWN MOWER

The first lawn mower was invented in England in 1827 and things have come a long way since then. Most are now powered by electric or small petrol engines.

SPRINKLER

Points: 10

Sprinklers are usually used to water lawns and flower beds when there hasn't been much rain. It can be great fun to play in the water too, as long as you don't mind getting very wet!

Points: 15

STRING OF ONIONS

These look quite charming and rustic hanging in a shed or kitchen. Hanging them is a good way to prevent them getting damp and rotting.

LEAF BLOWER

Points: 15

This is one of those tools that makes you wonder how you ever managed without it! It makes a lot of noise but saves hours of backbreaking raking.

Points: 5
for any type of rake

RAKE

This is the tool that will remove large stones and clumps from the soil, making it fine enough for planting tiny seeds into. Other rakes, like leaf rakes or spring tine rakes, are used for gathering leaves, dead grass and moss.

TROWEL

Points: 5

This hand tool is used for lifting plants and small amounts of soil. It is very versatile and can be used when potting up plants in the greenhouse and planting out seedlings in the garden.

Points: 5

HOE

Several different types of hoe have been developed, each for specific purposes. This draw hoe will be great for removing weeds between rows in the vegetable patch.

RIDE-ON MOWER

Top Spot!   Points: 30

If you have a large garden, you may need a ride-on mower. This kind of machine makes mowing a pleasure. Some have implements such as snow ploughs or trailers attached.

STRIMMER

Points: 10

Much quicker and more thorough than the old-fashioned long-handled shears, strimmers are used to trim the long grass at the edge of a lawn.

Points: 5

WATERING CAN

The fine spray is excellent for watering seedlings. On the rare occasion we have a long hot summer, this is a vital tool for the gardener.

SHEARS

Points: 5

Shears are a very handy tool not only to keep the hedge neat and tidy but they can also cut the grass where the mower can't quite reach.

Points: 5

Whether your garden contains flowers, vegetables or both, at some time or other you are going to need a spade to dig the soil.

FORK

Points: 5

The frequent gardener will appreciate a sturdy, well-balanced fork. A good fork will easily break clods of earth into smaller pieces. It is also better than a spade for digging up potatoes as it's less likely to cause them damage.

SHOVEL

Points: 10

A vital tool when you need to shift large quantities of bulky material such as compost. It is not designed for digging.

Points: 10

SECATEURS

There are different types of secateurs, each for a very specific job. This type - called bypass secateurs - are the most common and are mainly used for pruning shrubs and trees.

PRUNING SAW

Points: 15

The curved blade of this saw cuts on the pulling stroke. Great for cutting medium-sized branches, it can also be attached to an extension pole to prune high up branches.

Points: 5

DANDELION

Relied on for food by many insects that come out of hibernation early in the year, they are a weed that is hard to get rid of due to their long taproot. The young leaves can be used in salads or infused to make tea and the roots can be made into a passable coffee substitute.

GROUND ELDER

Points: 5

Tenacious is a good word to use when describing this plant. It never gives up and will grow a whole new plant from the tiniest part left in the soil after weeding.

Points: 5

NETTLE

Nettles are a good sign of fertile ground but they can be hard to get rid of. You can eat them when steamed or they can be turned into soup but make sure you pick them with gloves on!

HORSETAIL

Points: 10

This is the only survivor of a group of plants that has been around for over 100 million years! Dinosaurs would have grazed on it and other plants of the species that would have reached 30m (98ft) in height. The weeds we find in our gardens are much smaller than that.

Points: 5

DAISY

Some gardeners don't like daisies because they think they spoil their lawns. Daisies are easy to find and, with a little patience, they can be made in to daisy chains.

Points: 5

BINDWEED

BINDWEED

Pretty flowers maybe, but try to get rid of them and they become a problem. Every broken piece of root becomes a whole new plant, and they 'bind' or wind themselves as they climb.

HOGWEED

Points: 10

There are about 60 species of hogweed, the most common of which reaches about 1.2m (4ft) but the giant hogweed can reach 5m (16ft)! Don't touch the giant variety if you come across it as it will give you a long-lasting and painful skin rash.

Points: 10

BROAD-LEAVED DOCK

This is very hard to get rid of as the roots go down 1.5m (5ft) into the soil. The dock is not all bad though – if you get stung by a nettle, rub a dock leaf onto the sting and you will soon forget that you were hurt.

Points: 15

THISTLE

The thistle has been the national emblem of Scotland since the reign of Alexander III in the 13th century.

Points: 10

CATERPILLAR

This is the larval form of moths and butterflies. Caterpillars gorge on host plants and then wrap themselves in a silk cocoon. While inside they change into the adult winged insect in a process called Metamorphosis. Amazing!

MOTH

Points: 10

There are thought to be nearly 2500 moth species in the UK – they come in many colours and sizes and, some are poisonous. Their complex colour schemes are designed to ward off predators, mainly birds.

Points: 5

SLUG

A slug is a gastropod without a shell. Most are harmless but a few do great damage in flower borders and vegetable patches.

APHID

Points: 5

There are more than 500 species of aphids in the world. These sap-sucking insect pests feed on foliage but some attack plant roots and they do untold damage to crops worldwide. Most gardeners refer to aphids by their more common name – greenflies.

Points: 5

SNAIL

Snails are capable of doing just as much damage as slugs. They come out at night and devour their chosen plant and then disappear before dawn into cracks in walls and under stones or logs.

SQUIRREL

Points: 10

He might look cute but this grey squirrel is really a villain. They carry a disease called squirrel pox, which is wiping out our native red squirrel, as well as causing damage to large numbers of trees.

Points: 10

SEED PACKET

Buying a packet of seeds is a great way to start growing plants. They are normally presented in an eye-catching display so you'll be sure to spot them. Choose what type you want and see the result of your hard work when the seeds start to germinate!

SEEDLING

Points: 10

As a result of the gardener's patience and a little help from the weather, the seeds have finally germinated and are well on their way to becoming full-sized plants.

TROPICAL FISH

Points: 15

It is now quite common for garden centres to have a specialist aquarium section. Many fish are wonderfully coloured and watching them is very relaxing. Keeping tropical fish can be difficult but the results will be well worth the hard work.

Points: 10

GROWBAG

Growbags are a cheap and versatile means of extending your garden. With a little knowledge and some dedication anyone can grow their own tomatoes, strawberries or lettuces in a growbag full of compost.

COMPOST

Points: 10

Compost has been made commercially for years and is sold in tough plastic sacks. Keen gardeners often make their own compost from vegetable scraps, leaves and other organic matter.

Points: 35   **Top Spot!**   **BADGER**

We tend to think that badgers are woodland animals, living in setts in the countryside. However, they easily adapt to urban life and colonies have been found in the counties of Surrey, Sussex and Yorkshire, to name just a few.

CAT

Points: 5

For most of the day (and most of the night) most cats are asleep but when they wake up they become like tigers, hunting prey like mice and birds in the garden just like a wild animal.

Points: 20

FOX

This is a real wild animal! Foxes are known for their cunning and have colonised some towns completely, helped by some people feeding them on a regular basis.

CHICKEN

Points: 15

Not quite visitors and not quite pets! Looking after your own small flock is a very rewarding pastime and of course you get fresh eggs every day.

Points: 10

LADYBIRD

Ladybirds are voracious predators and definitely the gardener's friend as they eat scale insects and aphids. There is no truth in the myth that the more spots, the older the insect!

BEETLE

Points: 10

Beetles have been on earth for at least 300 million years. In that time they have colonised every type of habitat, some even living on and under water. There are now over 300,000 species of beetle.

Points: 10

HONEY BEE

Without the humble honey bee our cupboards, fridges and freezers would be half-empty! We often don't appreciate what a vital job bees do with the pollination of flowers, especially those of fruit trees and shrubs.

SPIDER

Points: 5

In spite of what you may think, spiders are doing us all a favour! Their webs catch all sorts of insects which the spider then eats. Without them our gardens and houses would be overrun with insect pests.

 Points: 5

WORM

Earthworms are the unseen heroes of the garden. They recycle dead leaves, excavate tunnels which aerate the soil and at the same time help with drainage. All these activities benefit our flowers, vegetables and trees.

RED ADMIRAL

Points: 20

Butterflies are regular visitors to gardens in the summer months especially gardens with lots of grasses and flowers. The red admiral is a large butterfly that can be seen in the garden at almost any time of the year, particularly if you have ivy.

Points: 30   Top Spot!   **HEDGEHOG**

If you go to the back door to call in your cat for the night, you may well hear something snuffling in the flower beds. Don't be alarmed, it's not a giant beast just a hungry hedgehog looking for snails and slugs.

BEEHIVE

Points: 20

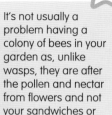

It's not usually a problem having a colony of bees in your garden as, unlike wasps, they are after the pollen and nectar from flowers and not your sandwiches or fizzy drinks.

Points: 10

BIRD BATH

Not only do birds need fresh, clean water to drink, they also need it to bathe in. It's absolutely vital that they keep their feathers clean. A nice clean, shallow bath quite close to some bushes where they can hide and preen will be just perfect.

BIRD FEEDER

Points: 5

5

Hanging a feeder in a tree gives birds somewhere safe to feed. There are special feeders for different types of seeds, peanuts or fat balls, and these all attract different types of birds. Cleaning the feeder regularly will help stop diseases being passed on.

10

Points: 10

BIRD TABLE

Some birds, such as robins, prefer to feed from a table than from a feeder. Bread can be bad for birds so it's best to feed them seeds, peanuts, meal worms, or even chopped up bacon rind.

Points: 10

NESTING BOX

Placing a nesting box high up in a tree or on a wall will provide a place for small birds to lay their eggs and rear their young safe from predators. After the baby birds have fledged, a small mammal might move in for the winter.

BUG HOUSE

Points: 15

A bug house filled with cut down bamboo cane, bundles of twigs or pine cones provides shelter for beneficial garden insects such as spiders, lacewings and ladybirds. Bees and butterflies might also hibernate in them. If you have enough space you could make a bug hotel!

Points: 5

GATE

Gates help to make our gardens secure and are especially useful if you have a dog. They are usually made of wood or metal and some can be very ornate. Electric gates open and close automatically.

FENCING

Points: 5

Fences are used to create a boundary between properties or just create definition between different areas of the same garden. They are made of iron or wood and can be quite decorative.

Points: 10

STONE WALLING

Using stone to form a boundary wall is a practice that has gone on for thousands of years. This type of wall provides numerous nooks and crannies for plants to grow and insects to hide in.

WASHING LINE

Points: 5

Washing lines can be a single cord stretched across the garden, or a rotary style which goes round in the breeze. Clothes are attached to the line with pegs so they can dry in the sun.

Points: 5

DECKING

Wooden decking is often raised up above the level of the lawn and is a very relaxing place to sit and enjoy the garden.

GRAVEL DRIVE

Points: 15

As long as you are prepared to weed occasionally, gravel looks very smart, natural and even sounds nice and scrunchy when you walk on it!

Points: 10

FOUNTAIN

The sound of water falling from a fountain into a pool is very relaxing and reminds us of a family day out, sitting on a river bank fishing or maybe having a family picnic.

STATUE

Points: 10

Statues tend to be carved from blocks of stone or cast of metal, of which bronze is the most common. The subjects can vary from animals to mythical figures. They are often used to provide a focal point in the garden.

BONSAI

Points: 20

This is the ancient far-eastern practice of growing miniaturised trees in containers. The plants are fussed over by their owners who constantly monitor every aspect of their life. These trees can be hundreds of years old and cost hundreds of pounds!

Points: 5

UNUSUAL CONTAINER

This is quaint and pretty way to recycle your old boots when they wear out or just start to leak! Make sure that they do have a few holes in the soles for drainage or your plants will drown.

Points: 5

PLANT CONTAINER

What better way to show off a valued and beautiful flowering plant than by using a contrasting coloured container. They can be made of plastic or pottery and are available in a wide variety of shapes and colours.

CACTUS

Points: 15

Cactus plants are not as hard to grow as is thought, and it's not true that they only flower every seven years! Most of the time they are kept indoors but during dry weather there is no reason why they can't be outside in the sun and fresh air.

Points: 5

FLOWER POT

They can be made of high density plastic or terracotta, which is a type of pottery. The most common types vary in size from 5cm (2 inches) to 30cm (12 inches) in diameter. Special giant ones are available which can hold 500 litres of compost.

WATER WELL

Points: 15

Most modern water wells are just for ornamental purposes and contain very little water. People often throw money into large water wells to try and make a wish come true.

 Points: 15

GARDEN GNOME

Garden gnomes were first made by a German potter in response to a local myth about a gnome's willingness to help in the garden at night. They were introduced to England in 1847 and are still popular today.

PARASOL

Points: 15

A perfect way to keep cool on a hot day, a parasol will also offer some protection from the sun and help in keeping your food and drinks cool.

Points: 10

HOME-MADE COMPOST

A compost bin can be made of wood or plastic and should be sited away from the house. Just keep topping it up with kitchen peelings, some hedge clippings and a little grass and very soon you will have your own home-made compost, which can be used to enrich the soil.

RECYCLING BIN

Points: 5

These special bins are provided by the local councils to help us recycle all sorts of different materials. Check carefully, they are not all green and they are not all this shape.

Points: 10

WATER BUTT

Rainwater is collected from the roof of your house using gutters and pipes, and is better for your plants than tap water. If your house is fitted with a water meter, a butt will save money too!

POND

Points: 10

With a pond in the garden you will be able to spot all types of creatures arriving for a drink or a bath. It doesn't have to be large – all standing water is appreciated by nature, just remember to remove the fallen leaves in autumn and keep it topped up with water.

Points: 15

GOLDFISH

Goldfish usually grow much bigger in a pond than they would in a fish tank because they have a lot more space, and can reach lengths of over 20cm (8 inches). They are a kind of carp and can range in colour from red to yellow.

Points: 10

WATER LILY

Water lilies are actually plants that have their roots in mud at the bottom of the pond and their flowers and leaves up on the surface. The flowers are often white or pink.

TOAD

Points: 15

The common toad is mostly nocturnal and hides in sheltered places during the day. They are broad and squat with warty skin. To deter predators, they secrete an irritant from their skin.

Points: 15

FROGSPAWN

Frogs are getting much rarer so if you see frogspawn leave it in the pond and watch to see it hatch into tadpoles, which will then change into froglets.

INDEX

i-SPY

How to get your i-SPY certificate and badge

Let us know when you've become a super-spotter with 1000 points and we'll send you a special certificate and badge!

HERE'S WHAT TO DO!

✓ Ask an adult to check your score.

✓ Visit www.collins.co.uk/i-SPY to apply for your certificate. If you are under the age of 13 you will need a parent or guardian to do this.

✓ We'll send your certificate via email and you'll receive a brilliant badge through the post!